بسم الله الرحمن الرحيم

FATIMAH IS ALI

stories from life of lady fatimah
(s) and imam ali (a)

ALI QAHRAMANI

Orignially published in Persian under the title
fatemeh ali ast by Kitabe Jamkaran.

ISBN 978-93-340-6940-2

CONTENTS

Birth of Two Lights

Union of Two Seas

Story of their Life

SECTION ONE

Birth
of
Two Lights

Birth in the Kaaba

A woman rushed ahead of the crowd, clasping herself to the Kaaba's curtains, and said:

"O Lord! I believe in You, the prophets, and the books You have sent. I confirm the words of Your friend Ibrahim al-Khalil, and I believe he built this sacred house. By the right of this child, I carry in my womb, make my pregnancy easy!"

And a miraculous event occurred! The wall of the house of Allah split open.

The crowd ran towards the Kaaba, but the wall closed, and no matter what they did, the walls did not open.

Four days later, on the 13th of Rajab 599 AD (30 years after the Holy Prophet's birth), the wall split open again from the same spot. Fatimah bint Asad was returning from the Divine banquet, holding her son Ali.

2

The Scent of Prophethood

The responsibility of caring for Ali fell upon the Holy Prophet of Islam. His childhood was embraced in the warmth and loving home of the Prophet, and the Messenger of Allah took charge of his upbringing.

Throughout all this time, never did Ali utter a falsehood in speech or commit any mistake in his actions, and the Messenger witnessed nothing from Ali except truthfulness and righteousness.

The heavenly nature of the Prophet had made Ali, enlightened and spiritual. Ali saw the light of revelation and prophecy and smelled the scent of prophethood.

God had placed a light within the embrace of another light.

3

Eternal Affection

Since the day he took responsibility of Ali's upbringing, he looked after him like a loving mother. He would constantly hug him, put him in his own room, and lay him in his special bed. At times, he would lovingly feed him, putting each morsel into his mouth with care.

Ali recognized himself in the embrace of love. Like a child constantly by his mother's side, he was always with him and never left him alone.

Every day, the Prophet showed Ali fresh signs of his noble character and asked Ali to follow his example.

Rough Terrain

The path was a bit rough, and walking it was a little challenging. Once you left the city, you had to trek a long distance to reach the foot of the mountain. The relatively steep slope made the journey difficult. At the top of the hill, the entrance to a cave was situated. Sometimes, Ali would accompany him on the path towards the cave.

In this cave, Ali was the only confidant of the Prophet. The solitude of the Prophet's secret conversations belonged to Ali, and the companion of Ali's solitude was the Prophet.

Solitude in the Cave of Hira

When the men of Mecca became weary of the worldly ways, they sought the path to Hira, where they would spend long stretches in solitude, seeking closeness to Allah. Throughout this time, the Cave of Hira was not just a shelter but a sanctuary, soon to be visited by the angel of revelation. Climbing mountains and seeking seclusion was a custom from the days of *jahiliyyah* before the Prophet's time. During these moments, the only companion who saw him and communicated with him was the young Ali.

In those days, it was Ali who brought food and water from Mecca for the Prophet, conveying news from the city. And when revelation descended, it was Ali who stood by the Prophet's side.

6

Only These Three

He was a perfume merchant whose job was trading and traveling and he often went to Mecca.

One afternoon, he sat with his old friends beside the Kaaba. A man with a beautiful face passed by them. He stood beside the Kaaba. Then a young man joined him, and then a woman stood behind them. All of them bent down. Then they prostrated on the ground.

Seeing these three and their humble worship was refreshing for him, even though he did not recognize them. This man said in amazement, "What a remarkable incident!"

The host of this gathering was Abbas, the son of Abd al-Muttalib. He introduced them one by one:

"The first is my cousin Muhammad, the son of Abd Allah. And the other is Ali, the son of my

other cousin Abu Talib. The third is the wife of
Muhammad. This man claims to be the messenger of the Lord, and until today, only these
two have believed in him; Khadijah and Ali."

Warning to the Closest Relatives

It seemed like his eyes, filled with anticipation and concern, were stitched to the sky of Divine mercy. He longed for the arrival of his dearest heavenly friend. Three years had passed since his first formal meeting with the angel of revelation, twenty years before the incident of Saqifah.

A gentle breeze, filled with affection, began to blow. The scent of a friend was in the air. From the fragrance that pervaded the space, he understood that his prayers and moments of anticipation had been answered.

Once again, the Divine messenger came with good news in the presence of the Prophet. It was decreed that the position of *khilafah* and succession to the Holy Prophet should be determined. The angel began to speak: "And warn your closest relatives; O Prophet! Ali will be your vizier (*vazir*), successor (*wasi*), and deputy (*khalifah*) after you."

The Second Gathering

The guests had gathered again. Among the invitees were people who could eat a substantial portion of camel's meat; however, they were very surprised to see that for forty guests, only a lamb leg, some bread, and some milk had been prepared.

They mocked and laughed. They said, "He hasn't even prepared enough food for one of us!" But surprisingly everyone ate, and there was enough food.

It was the second gathering. The Holy Prophet didn't allow people like Abu Lahab to turn the gathering into a gathering of play and merrymaking like last time.

He stood up and said, "The key to both worldly and hereafter happiness lies in two things; belief in the oneness of God and my prophethood." He paused and continued,

"Whoever supports me and helps me, will be my brother, vizier, successor, and *khalifah* after me." After repeating this request three times, no one except Ali ibn Abi Talib stood up to support him and give him an affirmative answer.

Facing the crowd, he said, "Ali is my brother, successor, and *khalifah* among you."

As they were leaving, uncles and cousins mocked Abu Talib, saying, "Now after Muhammad, you would have to also listen to your son Ali!"

What I see, you see as well

Ali, as always, was respectfully seated with the Messenger of Allah. Suddenly, a serene and spiritual feeling enveloped the Prophet of God. From the luminosity of his countenance, one could discern a Divine matter had occurred. Usually, when revelation descended upon him, this radiance would manifest on his blessed face.

At this moment, strange cries and wails were heard. Ali asked, "O Messenger of God! Whose cries are these?" He replied, "It is Satan! The wails you heard are because he has despaired of being worshipped [and obeyed] by human beings."

Then he continued, "O Ali, what I hear, you hear, and what I see, you see, except that you are not a prophet; rather, you are my vizier and deputy, walking in the path of purity and goodness."

10

The Great Reward

It had never happened before that he would leave without informing anyone, but this time it seemed he had no intention of coming or giving any news of his whereabouts. Khadijah, despite her strength of character, was deeply troubled. She feared that the unbelievers of Quraysh might have caused him harm. On her prayer mat, she found the best solace for the restlessness of her heart through communion with the Creator.

A voice came from outside. Ali, the messenger of Muhammad, brought some joyful news. He said: "The Messenger of God is alive and in perfect health. He sends his greetings and says: Forgive me. It was not in my hands, otherwise I would have informed you. It is God's command that I stay away from you for a while. Value this opportunity and engage in worship. A great reward from the Creator awaits you on this path."

Meeting with the One Lord

Whenever he wanted to receive great spiritual gifts from Allah, he would seclude himself for a number of nights. This was God's secret with the Messenger, but this last retreat was different; this time he wasn't supposed to spend it outside the city in solitude and prayer. It was a great blessing that Allah had ordained his seclusion to be in the house of Abu Talib for forty days. He would spend this time in prayer, supplication, and worship whilst Ali accompanied him.

Those special days were coming to an end when the angle came carrying a message from Allah with great joy and delight. It was now the time for Ahmad to witness the beauty of the One Lord.

12

Heavenly Fruit

An angel arrived earlier. It stood beside a beautiful and magnificent tree. The heavenly fragrance of the fruit on the tree, carried by the breeze mesmerized anyone nearby. The beauty of the spiritual realm is all-encompassing, but the freshness, beauty, and sweet scent of this tree were something else entirely. The angel said to the Messenger of Allah, "This is the tree from which you must eat. God has willed to grant you, from this fruit, a *houri* in the form of a human being."

In this Divine spiritual banquet, they presented the reward of absolute goodness, purity, and servitude to the Prophet in its most complete form.

13

Companion of the Mother

In her loneliness, Khadijah had buried all the sorrows in her heart. She knelt by the corner, lost in her memories. The days when the women of Mecca longed to be with her had passed before her eyes. It had been a long time no one had come to visit her.

She heard a whisper, "My dear mother, do not be sad! Allah the Exalted is the support and the refuge of my beloved father." She looked around fearfully. She realized the voice was from within her. The child she carried in her womb was comforting the mother.

14

Loneliness

In the last days of the initial months of the fifth year of the Prophet's mission, Khadijah spent her days in loneliness. The time for her pregnancy arrived, and Khadijah sent for some women from the Quraysh to assist her, but none of them came. They left her alone. They conveyed the message: "We had warned you of this day when we told you not to marry Muhammad."

Khadijah's heart shattered. It was a tough period. She curled up in pain. There was no one to help her. Even her friends had deserted her; however, she did not lose hope in God. She knew that God was sufficient for her.

15

The Four Heavenly Ladies

Khadijah, burdened with pain and anguish, glanced at the door to see if anyone was by her side. Her maid, with much embarrassment, came forward and said:

"My lady! The women of Mecca, your old friends, those past companions, have left you alone."

Khadijah, having lost hope in any help from the people, and in a state where her heart weighed with sorrow, saw the doors of heaven open, and a cascade of light shone upon her modest house.

The four Divine ladies, accompanied by a host of houris and angels, rushed to aid the noble Khadijah.

16

The Birth of Fatimah

Four lofty, dignified women entered the room, their presence commanding respect. Khadijah looked up in amazement.

One of them spoke gently, "Fear not! We come from God to aid you. I am Sarah, the wife of Ibrahim. Beside me stands Asiya, the wife of Fir'aun, and to her right is Maryam, the mother of Isa. And the fourth is Kulthum, the sister of Musa."

With their help, the child came into the world. They bathed him with the water of Kawthar. Then the new-born spoke, "I bear witness that there is no god but Allah, and Muhammad is the Messenger of Allah, the leader of the prophets, and Ali is the leader of the *awsiya*, and my offspring are the chiefs of the people."

She then greeted all the heavenly women, each one by their name.

Mother of her father

One year had passed from the night when the termites ate up all the treaties of the polytheists stored in Kaaba except the word 'Allah'. The siege on the Muslims, from all cultural, political, social, and economic aspects, was lifted, and everything seemed to return to normal when suddenly everything fell apart again. The Prophet's uncle Abu Talib departed from this world towards the destination of paradise.

Likewise, it wasn't long before the angel of death came to take mother of Zahra, the daughter of the Prophet, to paradise. Now Fatimah, who was only five springs old, was becoming a mother to her father.

18

Fatimah is the mercy of God.

Her father kissed her hands and forehead with love, not caring about the looks or judgments of others. He didn't hide this affection from anyone.

At a time when Arabs would insult daughters, he considered having a daughter as a source of pride and boasted about having been blessed with one by God. In the eyes of the Messenger of Mercy, a son was considered God's blessings and a daughter was likened to Divine mercy.

The beloved Messenger of Islam wouldn't sleep until he had kissed the radiant face of Fatimah.

The Noble Lady

She was very knowledgeable and polite, always smiling and kind; a perfect example of a faithful woman. Jibra'il had given the glad tidings of her heavenly status years before she left the world. The Prophet used to call her Umm Salamah.

She would say: "After the Messenger of God united me in marriage, he entrusted me with Fatimah the Pure to nurture her. I spared no effort, and I poured everything I had into raising Fatimah. But I swear by God! She was much more polite and knowledgeable than me."

20

The Foremost of Women

Beauty and adornment of outwardly appearance are one matter, and the goodness of character and inner virtues are another. But a true marvel arises when these qualities converge in one person!

The beauty of her character added to the grace of her countenance. She was entirely beautiful, and her beauty was all-encompassing!

Her father, the Seal of the Prophets, would say about her: "If all the beauties and perfections of humanity were to be gathered in one person, surely they would manifest in Fatimah. My daughter Fatimah surpasses all in the manifestation of beauty and goodness, and in terms of lineage and nobility, she is the best among the people of the earth."

And he would say: "Fatimah, my dear! It is enough of an honour for you that among the women of intellect and dignity of the world, such as Mary, Khadijah, and Asiyah, you stand foremost among them."

21

The First Idol Breaker

When the earth wrapped itself in the night's cloak and drowned in sleep, he called me forth. As I arrived at Lady Khadijah's house, he said, "Ali, come with me."

In the dark and narrow alleys of Mecca, I followed him step by step. The hustle and bustle of the narrow alleys had come to an end. I saw him standing in front of the Kaaba. The usual commotion of the city was nowhere to be seen. The Messenger of Allah, with humility, said, "Come up from my shoulder!" Then he bowed. I, having said "Labbayk," went up from his blessed shoulder. When I reached the roof of the Kaaba, whatever idols there were, I smashed them.

When I came down, he said, "The first person to break idols was your forefather Ibrahim al-Khalil, and after him, you are the first idol breaker!"

22

Risking his own Life

They said, "Imprison him! So that these words and thoughts are removed from his mind!"

They said, "Exile him far away so that we can be safe from his actions and words!"

They said, "Eliminate him!"

Everyone agreed to this last suggestion and they were determined that a group of swordsmen would raid his house at night and finish him off while he slept.

Jibra'il, along with God's greetings, informed the Prophet about the plan of the polytheists. The Prophet himself had to leave the house at the beginning of the night, and someone resembling him would sleep in his bed to confuse the attackers. Ali risked his life for this!

It was midnight when the polytheists decided to finish the job with their sudden attack…

It was still before dawn when Jibra'il descended from the heavens again with glad tidings and heavenly verses: "And among the people is he who sells his soul seeking the pleasure of Allah, and Allah is most kind to [His] servants." (2:207)

23

You have hurt me

When Amr entered the mosque, he felt the weight of the Prophet's gaze, which seemed to be fixated onto him.

He wondered to himself, "What could have caused the Messenger of God to be upset with me like this? No matter how much he thought about it, nothing came to mind."

Without prelude, the Prophet said, "Oh Amr! By God, you have hurt me. Why? Because you have hurt Ali. And whoever hurts him, has hurt me."

24

The Devoted Servant

"Oh God! I beseech you, by your most beloved servants, to have mercy on the sinners at your doorstep. O Lord! I implore you, by your closest servants... O Creator! I call upon you through Ali..."

Ayesha heard these supplications from the Prophet and after the prayer, she asked, "Doesn't God have lofty angels or esteemed prophets like you, whom one could call upon for the forgiveness of the sins of his people, instead of asking by the name of Ali?"

In response, the Prophet said, "In all that I have observed in the kingdom of God, I have not found any servants superior to Ali, by whose station I could ask Allah."

The Most Similar

She seemed like the Prophet; her actions, her speech, and even the tone of her words; and that is how much she was close to him. Ayesha described her: "I have never seen anyone more similar to the Prophet in speech than Fatimah. When she would enter, her father would welcome her with an incomparably affectionate welcome. He would kiss her hands many times and would make her sit in his own place.

Likewise, whenever the Prophet entered upon Fatimah, she would stand up respectfully in front of her father and warmly welcome him, kissing his hands."

26

Hajj and Recitation of the Entire Quran

Her bed was spread out. Her father sought permission and entered the room. When he saw his daughter, he said, "My dear! Do not sleep unless you have done four things: recite the entire Quran; please the believers and make the prophets intercede for you; also, perform Hajj and Umrah."

He said this and stood to pray.

The daughter, who had become curious hearing these words, patiently waited until her father finished praying.

"Dear father! You have burdened me with four things, while I am not capable of doing any," she said.

Her father smiled and said, "When you recite Surah al-Ikhlas three times, it is as if you have completed the Quran. Likewise, when you send blessings upon me and the prophets before me, they will intercede for you on the Day of Judgment. Additionally, when you seek forgiveness for the believers, they will all be pleased with you. And when you say Subhan Allah, al-Hamd li-Allah, La ilaha illa Allah, and Allah Akbar, it is as if you have performed Hajj and Umrah."

27

The Light

Her hands were always raised in prayer. She entrusted everyone to prayer. She would say, "Even salt for food and even the lace of shoes must be asked from God." She was tireless in her work and efforts. She detested idleness and being idle. She kissed the hands of hard-working labourers. She considered prayer the essence of worship and the root of servitude. Above all, she advised her daughter to strive and pray. In her view, the sweetness of life was in work and its blessings in prayer.

Fatimah, who stood for prayer, opening her hands of supplication to the angels and illuminating, the angels called this earthly light "Zahra."

28

Bravery

Near a small village, halfway between Mecca and Medina, in the month of Ramadan of the second year after Hijra, the first official battle of Islam against disbelief took place.

The son of Abu Talib carried the black flag of Islam. Despite their small number and lack of suitable preparation, Muslims, with Divine assistance, emerged victorious over the fully armed army of the Quraysh. The battle was one of bravery and steadfastness, but Ali's steadfastness in the midst of the battlefield was exemplary. At the end of the battle, he registered most of the enemy casualties under his own name.

Union
of
Two Seas

29

Affection

"I offer one hundred black camels, adorned with Egyptian silk, and ten thousand gold dinars as the dowry for Fatimah. Give her to me," said Abd al-Rahman bin Auf.

Uthman stepped forward, "I offer the same dowry, with the only difference being that I became a Muslim sooner and have better intentions than Abd al-Rahman."

The Prophet was not pleased. He turned to them, and said, "Do you think I am a slave to money and wealth, or perhaps you assume marriage is a matter of trade?! The choice of Fatimah's spouse lies with God."

This was the answer he had given to Abu Bakr and others before. He made it clear to everyone that the criterion for any action, even the choice of a life partner, is the pleasure of God.

30

Only Ali

People would gather on the platforms around the mosque courtyard at midday. The latest events in Medina and news from Arabia were usually their main topics of discussion, but that day, their conversations were scattered. Death, accidents, marriages, etc. The thread of conversation was interrupted when news about the Prophet's daughter reached them. In an instant, all eyes turned to each other trying to understand what had happened. They whispered to themselves that now that everyone had heard the rejection of many proposals, the Prophet had surely chosen Ali for his only daughter.

They said, "How wonderful it would be if Ali took the lead as well. If there's a turn to be taken, it's Ali's turn to seek his fate in marrying Fatimah."

31

Seeking Fatimah's Hand

He wasn't at home. Nor he was in the city. Someone from the date palm orchard of one of the Ansar brought news of him. He was watering the orchard with the help of his camel, giving water to the trees. They approached him and asked:

"Why aren't you getting married?! Everyone is taking their proposals for Fatimah to the Holy Prophet. Why aren't you going to the Prophet's house?"

"What's happened that you've come to me? Why are you insisting that I take the lead?"

"All those who proposed have received a negative answer. You are the only one whom the Prophet, because of his deep affection for you, would accept."

32

Who is Better than You?

He thrust the shovel he held into the ground. His gaze, filled with shyness and hope, fell to the earth.

"I would not hide anything from you! Marrying someone like Fatimah is an honour for me too! My silence is not from shyness, but from the fear of being prevented from achieving my wish."

They said, "Where will the Prophet find someone like you? If he doesn't give Fatimah to you, then who does he intend to marry her to? While you are the closest person to her and the most superior of his Ummah."

33

An Important Decision

Since childhood, Imam Ali was raised in the house of the Prophet. His blessed hands were Imam Ali's guide. The Prophet loved him like his own children, just like Fatimah. Imam Ali was aware of the Prophet's immense love for him, and this made his decision harder.

On one hand, poverty prevented him from going, but on the other hand, he knew that he couldn't find anyone equal to Fatimah in moral and spiritual virtues.

34

The Blessed Voice

The sound of knocking carried a message of good tidings and blessings. Prophet told Umm Salamah, "Please go and open the door! This is someone whom God and His Messenger love."

"Who is this man that the messenger is praising before even meeting him?"

"He is a man who doesn't falter or weaken in the face of difficulties. He is a friend, a brother, and the most beloved among people to me."

Eager to see and recognize this beloved man of God, Umm Salamah hurried towards the door.

Later, she said to Fatimah, "Such eagerness to recognize this beloved of the Messenger of God overcame me that when I got up to open the door, I was close to stumbling. When I opened the door, my eyes lit up at the sight of Ali's radiant face."

35

Modesty and Shyness

Since he arrived, he did not raise his head for a moment. Out of modesty and shyness, he it was difficult for him to speak.

A gentle voice brought him closer:

"It seems you have something to say? Don't be shy! Speak from your heart."

"May my parents be sacrificed for you! I have grown up in your house. You have strived in my upbringing for years, and by the grace of your existence, I have flourished. I have nothing of the world's wealth, but you are my treasure in this world and the Hereafter. The time for my marriage has come, and I can't find a more suitable wife than your daughter. This is all I desire."

The father went towards Fatimah's room.

36

Silent Approval

The Prophet took slow and measured steps, as usual. The father approached the door of his beloved daughter's room, gently knocking a few times. Zahra was accustomed to this sound which served as a sign of kindness and affection.

He sought permission and entered. Zahra stood up as a sign of respect and took her father's cloak. She fetched water and washed her blessed father's feet.

Then, she performed *wudhu* and sat in her father's presence.

"My daughter! Today's what I want to speak is unlike other conversations. I want to talk to you about my brother and my successor Ali. His virtue and position in Islam are undeniable. I have prayed to God to bring you together with the best of His creations, and now he has come to propose to you. I have come to ask for your opinion about Ali."

A mixture of shyness and happiness appeared on Fatimah's face. She remained silent. The Messenger of God stood up and exclaimed, "Allah Akbar, silence is a form of approval; yes, indeed. My daughter's silence indicates her approval."

The Request for Marriage

Even the thought of hearing a negative answer was difficult, although it was unlikely from someone lie Zahra that she would reject Ali.

Ali waited patiently to hear the response of the Prophet's daughter from the words of the Messenger of Allah.

The Prophet entered with a smile and a happy face.

Ali, unable to contain his happiness, said, "Greetings and blessings of God be upon you, who have always been kind-hearted, praised, and a source of blessings!"

38

Light upon Light

It was the command of the Almighty: "Pure women for pure men, and pure men for pure women." (24:26)

Those who came with proposals for Zahra were numerous, and their insistence was abundant, but among them, none were suitable for Fatimah until the son of Abu Talib stepped forward.

The Prophet was in the house of Umm Salamah when a special angle with immense majesty entered. He said, "I am Sarsa'il! The Lord has sent me to ask you to marry light with light."

The Prophet asked, "Who should marry whom?"

The angle replied, "Fatimah to Ali."

Then the Lord "merged the two seas, meeting each other." (55:19)

39

Companionship and Unity

There was never a day when proposals did not come for Fatimah, from every class, profession, and position. Fatimah had proposals who were wealthy, offering hefty dowries.

Despite all this, even with endless reproaches and abundant disapprovals from the women of Medina, she accepted the companionship, unity, and connection with Ali ibn Abi Talib.

Not for his wealth, for Ali had nothing of the worldly possessions, but for his lofty morals, spirituality, and his Godly noble soul.

40

The Dowry Price

The father's concern was expressed tenderly: "Do you have anything for marriage?"

"May my father and mother be sacrificed for you! Nothing of my life is hidden from you; I only have a sword, a shield, and a camel, which I use for fetching water."

He smiled and said, "Your sword is something essential; with it, you strive in the path of God. As for the camel, you need it for travel and household necessities; but I'll take the shield. Sell it and come to me."

The dowry of the noblest lady in the world was the price of a shield.

Selling the Shield

He rarely went to the market, except when required; when he had the need to buy or sell something.

He approached several people and sold the shield to the one who offered a fairer price.

He had no other business in the market. He quickly left the market to reach the luminous presence of the Divine Messenger sooner. He presented all the money at once. The Prophet gave some for preparing the wedding feast to Umm Salamah. He set aside some for buying bridal attire.

Simple Dowry

A large scarf, a white dress, four pillows, handmade rugs, a bed mat filled with date palm leaves, and dishes for food, all made of clay and pottery except for a copper pot.

When they brought Fatimah's dowry before the Messenger of God, his eyes became wet with tears. He turned his face towards the sky and said:

"O God, bless this wedding for those whose most of their utensils are made of clay!"

43

The Ceremony

The mosque couldn't accommodate any more guests; it was filled with wedding attendees. After the prayers, the marriage contract was recited; the marriage contract of Ali, the son of Abu Talib, and Fatimah, the daughter of Muhammad, the Messenger of God.

There was a strange murmuring. The Prophet began to speak, and everyone fell silent.

Before delivering the sermon, he said: "This honour belongs only to Fatimah, whose marriage contract was recited beforehand by Jibra'il, in the presence of a pure assembly of angels, in the fourth heaven."

"O people and O elders of Quraysh! I did not refuse your proposal for Fatimah; it was God who did not accept you. Jibra'il descended upon me and said: 'If I had not created Ali for Fatimah, there would have been no husband equal to Fatimah until the Day of Judgment.'

٤٤

The Marriage Contract

The Prophet conducted the marriage contract. Then, with his gestures, he called Ali forward. With radiant face and smile, Ali stood and said:

"I am infinitely grateful to God for His blessings, and I bear witness that there is no god but Him, and blessings upon His Messenger, Muhammad, whose rank and status He has exalted."

"O people! God has deemed marriage favourable for us and has commanded it. The Messenger of God, peace be upon him, brought Fatimah to me in marriage, and I have accepted her dowry."

The kind-hearted Prophet, with a smile of approval, prayed for their life together,

"May God bless them, protect them, and unite them. O God, bless them and make their union perpetual!"

45

Prepare Your Home

Tears welled up in his eyes. The mention of Khadijah brought back beautiful memories of their time together. He said, "Who could ever match Khadijah and fill her place for me? When people denied me and tormented me, she believed in me."

Then the Prophet (s) said, "Tell Ali to come so we can taste the sweetness of his words."

Ali came. The Prophet told him, "Prepare a home for your wife and yourself for celebration and joy."

It was as if the whole world had been given to him; he was extremely happy with these words.

The First Tenants

Ali didn't have much money to buy a house outright. Among the houses he had seen, the house of Harith ibn Nu'man had a better location and a more suitable price. This house that he had found was very small. However, neither the Prophet nor Fatimah minded the simplicity and modesty of the house. They rented the same house and it became the abode of their happiness.

When the master received the key to the house, he began preparing the necessities: clothes hangers, a water skin, pillows, a mat for bedding, a sack, handmade rugs, a sieve for flour, and a few pieces of crockery. They furnished the simplest yet most blessed home in Islam.

The best tenants in the Islamic world for a long time did not own a house.

47

The Union of Two Seas

The sun gathered its rays to spread them to every corner of the earth. The call to prayer was still a few minutes away. They brought the bride and groom to the house of Umm Salamah. The Prophet asked Umm Salamah to bring Fatimah.

Umm Salamah took Fatimah's hand, while her dress trailed on the ground, and sweat beaded on her forehead from shyness, she brought her before her father.

The Prophet prayed for her, "May God protect you in this world and the Hereafter!"

48

The Heavenly Garment

Jibra'il had swiftly arrived, accompanied by a host of angels. As always, he greeted with humility and bowed his head in respect before the Messenger of Allah. The Prophet was overjoyed to see the Divine messenger again and prepared himself to receive a message from God.

"O Messenger of the Almighty Lord! I come bearing greetings from our Lord to you and your noble household, Fatimah and Ali. In honour of this great blessing, God has sent a heavenly garment made of fine green silk for Fatimah's wedding."

49

The Simple Splendour

It was decided that the groom would invite some guests, and there would be relatives of the bride as well. The wedding was publicly announced at the mosque.

Hearts were filled with blossoms of joy and lips overflowed with the sound of *takbir* that wedding night.

Dinner was ready. They had also prepared sweets made from oil and dates. Both the meal and the sweets were simple but delightful.

The Prophet's wives attended to the women, and the friends of Ali looked after the men.

Most of the wedding guests were companions from the Suffah, the poorest among the people of Medina, both Muhajirun and Ansar.

This modest celebration was truly magnificent!

A Dua for the Newly-weds

The bride and groom entered their home hand in hand and sat quietly in a corner, waiting for the Prophet's arrival. Fatimah's eyes were modestly cast down due to shyness, and Ali too lowered his head.

After a short while, the revered father arrived. He asked Fatimah for a bowl of water and seated her beside him. He drank a sip from it, recited a *dua*, and then asked his daughter to come closer. For a blessing, he sprinkled some of the water over her. Then, he raised his hands in supplication: "O Lord! Here is my daughter, the dearest of all people to me. O God! And here is Ali, my brother, the most precious of all people to me. Lord, make him a *wali* and a leader of his people, and strengthen the bond of love within his household…"

This is how this blessed couple began the new chapter of their life.

Time by Heavenly Clock

It wasn't long since the Battle of Badr had ended. Ali had just returned from the expedition of Sawiq, sixteen days after the passing of Ruqayyah, the Prophet's daughter.

The union of these two paragons of virtue took place under such circumstances. Neither did the Prophet wait for the anniversary nor the forty days of mourning for his daughter, nor did anyone question the timing of the marriage.

Story

of

their Life

52

The Wedding Mat

The wedding caravan arrived at the groom's house. It was time for the bride to gracefully enter and light up the groom's home. The bride, a light herself, was entering a house as simple as any, carpeted with sand and furnished with only a few clay pots for water, a container for flour, a pillow, and a leather mat that served as their bed.

Their sleeping mat was a small quilt. If they covered themselves lengthwise, their sides would remain uncovered, and if used across, their heads and feet would not be covered. They were very poor, but even more so, they were grateful and content.

53

The Best Companion

Four days had passed since the marriage of Fatimah and Ali. Early in the morning, with a jug of milk in hand, the Holy Prophet made his way to his daughter and son-in-law's house.

He knocked on the door. The home was filled with joy at the sight of the father; the Prophet requested a bowl of water. He recited some verses of the Quran over it and blew into the water three times. Then, he offered a sip to Ali. He sprinkled the rest on Ali's chest and prayed, "May God keep you pure and clean from all impurity and unworthiness!"

He asked for water again and repeated the process for Fatimah. He asked, "Apple of my eyes, how do you find your husband?"

"Father, God has bestowed upon me the best of men."

The Prophet turned to Ali and asked, "O Ali! Now you speak how did you find your wife."

"She is the best companion and support in worshipping God."

54

Division of Work

It was the early days of their marriage, the beginning of their life together. They went to see the Prophet of God. The Prophet became their guide in managing the affairs of the house. When it came to discussing the household chores, the Prophet suggested: "Let Fatimah handle the works inside of the house, and Ali take care of the tasks outside the house."

A smile appeared on Fatimah's face, and she said, "God knows how happy I am with this arrangement!" The household tasks were not few, but Fatimah expressed her contentment, saying, "A woman's happiness lies in not being the subject of strangers' gazes without a suitable reason."

55

Housework

Grinding barley or wheat, baking bread, and preparing meals—all these tasks fell on Fatimah's shoulders. On one hand, she looked after the house, and on the other, she cared for and played with the children. Ali took care of fetching water, bringing firewood home, and doing the shopping; but he didn't just do tasks outside the house. Whenever he found the time, he would sweep the floors and help his beloved Fatimah with household chores.

One day, the Prophet was a guest at their house. The guest arrived earlier than expected and saw his daughter and son-in-law sitting together cleaning lentils. With a smile that showed his pleasure and happiness, he said, "God rewards a man who helps his wife with household chores with as many blessings as there are hairs on his body."

56

Lesson in Life

Their home was small, yet it was filled with vibrancy and blessings. Sometimes, when her husband was not at home, Fatimah's house became a gathering place and a centre for discussing religion and life.

She would sit with a group of women from Medina. They came to learn wisdom from the Prophet's daughter. After many questions and answers, everyone listened attentively. Fatimah taught them a lesson she had practised all her life with her husband: "The best among you is the one who is kindest and most gentle with others, and the most valuable among you is the one who is generous and kind to their spouse."

57

The Debate

Their argument escalated quite intensely. One was a believer, and the other was a disbeliever.

They said, "Let's go to the lady of the ladies of Medina." Each presented their case with arguments to support their views.

The believing woman was right. Fatimah confirmed her argument with logic and evidence, and did so kindly. The woman who won the debate was delighted with her victory.

Fatimah, with the sweetest smile in the world, said to the believing woman after the other lady had left, "The angels of God rejoice more for you, and Shaytan and his followers feel more sorrow than the sorrow of that disbelieving woman."

The Judge of the Contest

It was one of the first days that the children were practising their writing. Hasan and Husayn both wrote a line each and brought it to their mother. They wanted her to decide which one was better. Both lines were beautifully written. The mother said, "Go to your father and let him judge." Their father respected their effort and sent them to their grandfather, the Prophet of God. The revered grandfather left the decision to God's command.

God's command came: "Let Fatimah be the judge." Fatimah, obeying God's command, turned the qualitative contest into a quantitative one. She cut the string of her necklace and said, "Whoever collects more beads is the winner." Both children brought the same number of beads; thus, both were winners.

59

Raising the Next Generation

After the noon prayer ended, Ali went to see the Prophet to find out if there was any work that he needed to do. After being permitted to leave, he headed home. The distance from the mosque to his home was short. When he arrived, he began to recount the enriching sermon he had heard from the Messenger of God and the new revelations that Jibra'il had brought to the Prophet.

Fatimah, amidst the conversation, was confirming and completing the information before Ali even spoke. Surprised, Ali asked, "My dear Fatimah, were you at the mosque for the noon prayer today?"

Seeing the astonishment on Ali's face, Fatimah replied, "No, I prayed at home. When the children return from the prayer, they recount everything they learned in the presence of my father. They repeat and memorize the teachings they have heard."

This was how Fatimah raised her daughter, Zaynab, who became a narrator of Islamic narrations, protector, interpreter, and teacher of the Quran. After the tragedy of Karbala, Zaynab changed the Islamic world forever.

60

Hasan's Minbar

How could the grandson not resemble his grandfather, especially one who had conquered all the lofty peaks of humanity?

Hasan, who was blooming in the fifth spring of his life, had a daily routine; when he came home, he would sit high up like the Prophet and recount everything he had seen and heard from the Prophet in the mosque to his mother.

Father, having heard the story, eagerly awaited witnessing Hasan's zeal and wisdom. One day, he left the mosque earlier and came home. He hid in a corner of the house. Hasan entered and once again took his place on his daily *minbar*; but this time, his speech was not like usual. It seemed his tongue did not have its usual fluency. His mother was surprised. Hasan said, "Mother! I feel a heaviness. It is as if I am in the presence of a great and majestic person, and he is listening to my words. That is why my speech is not so eloquent."

At that moment, his father emerged from behind the curtain, embraced his son with a smile of approval, and kissed him.

61

Ocean of Affection

He would sit the children in his lap and kiss them. The children would climb all over him. With a laugh, he would seat them on his lap and with a smile, kiss their cheeks. Aqra' ibn Habis approached and said, "O Messenger of God! I have ten children; yet, I have never kissed any of them, nor have I shown the affection that you do."

The Messenger of Mercy became upset and said, "He who does not show mercy to the children and does not respect the elders is not one of us."

He had also taught Ali and Fatimah to be like himself: kind, patient, full of paternal and maternal love and affection.

62

Spiritual Upbringing

She paid attention to all aspects of upbringing, from manners and respect to social ethics. She knew that the most significant influence on children occurs when they see actions performed by adults. She saw all aspects of child upbringing in the spiritual dimension. She believed that if a person truly knew God and was pious, they would be ideal and flawless; for this reason, she placed greater importance on the spiritual upbringing of her children.

Her place of worship was in the home, visible to the children, and when she went to the mosque, she took the children with him. Ali was also his supporter in this method.

Fatimah and Ali had learned from the Prophet to always carry their beautiful children with them in the mosque and at their place of worship!

63

The Value of the Night of Qadr

From the start of the night, she stood in worship and prayer. It was the Night of Qadr, possibly the twenty-third night of the Holy month of Ramadhan.

From the day before, she had prepared the children, and they rested during the day. At the beginning of the night, she gave them just enough food so that they wouldn't feel sleepy from being too full. Between her prayers and supplications, she spoke kindly to the children to keep them alert and awake.

Occasionally, he would sprinkle a few drops of water on their faces like dew to refresh them for worship. She would say, "The truly deprived is one who misses out on the blessings of the Night of Qadr."

64

A Beautiful Name

When it comes to Zahra and Ali, a child's name reflects the family's values. So, when their first child was born, they called the grandfather to the bedside to help name him.

The great teacher of humanity taught them to choose a name beloved by God. It was decided that the angel of revelation would bring a beautiful name from God for the prophet's noble child. The name thus came from the presence of the One to Ahmad. He said, "God sends His greetings and commands: let this child be named 'Hasan' the beautiful."

The grandfather embraced the child, kissed him, and whispered the Adhan and Iqama in his ear, murmuring the child's name.

When Husayn and Zaynab were born, the story was much the same, and they chose beautiful, God-pleasing names for them too.

65

Lullaby

Father used to say, "The heart of a child is like empty land, and whatever seed is planted in it will grow." The father sowed the seeds of love and devotion to God in their hearts at the mosque and during religious ceremonies, and taught them to respect their mother on the way back home; the mother spoke of the father's status during the day and wove respect and love into her lullabies at bedtime for her children. Sometimes, she sang a special lullaby for Husayn, and sometimes, she recited for Hasan: "Dear Hasan! Be like your father. Release the truth from its chains. Worship the God of abundant grace and do not follow or befriend those who hold grudges."

Halal Laughter

Ali had come home early and was helping his wife with the chores. Fatimah attended to the household tasks. Then, it was time for playing and cuddling with the children. Amidst their playful activities, she taught them important life lessons.

Hasan's face resembled the moon more, while Husayn looked like his mother and grandfather. That day, besides healthy games and life lessons, the children also learned about kindness and halal laughter.

Hasan sat on his father's lap, and Husayn was in his mother's arms. Fatimah stroked Husayn and said with a smile, "You look like my father, not your father Ali."

Ali, delighted by Zahra's joke, cuddled Hasan and smiled happily, enjoying the joy of his family.

67

Children's Playmate

Whenever he visited his daughter's house, the children wouldn't let him sit still for a moment; he became their ride, and they enjoyed piggyback rides from their grandfather. Sometimes, he would lie on his back, placing the children on his chest, and tell them stories and anecdotes. At other times, he joined in their games.

The situation was similar when their father came home. Sometimes, they saw him helping their mother with household chores, and their playtime included helping their parents too.

The mother also often joined in their playful games and sometimes turned important practical lessons into stories. She would seat Hasan and Husayn on her lap and tell them stories about how to live a meaningful life and how to be a servant of Allah.

Hospitality

After the evening and night prayers, it was time for the sermon. During the Holy Prophet's sermon, a needy Arab man entered the mosque and complained of hunger and hardship. The Prophet gestured for the man to sit down.

A messenger was sent to the wives of the Prophet to fetch something for the man but he returned empty-handed. This time, the Prophet asked the Muslims to help the man so that he would not leave empty-handed. Everyone except Ali made excuses. Ali was no better off than the other Muslims, but he took the man's hand and brought him home.

Ali led the guest to the sitting room and then went inside to where Fatimah was. Without Ali saying anything, Fatimah read the whole story from his expression: "The children are also hungry, and we have nothing in the house

but a little food. I will entertain the children
and put them to bed; you serve the guest with
whatever we have."

69

The Story of Selflessness

The children were waiting for their dinner. As always, their mother entered the room with a smile. She said to the children, "Today we have a story of selflessness. Who will rush to Mother's embrace first?!"

Ali went to the guest room. This time, unusually, he did not light a lamp. He laid the table in the dark and placed the little food they had on it. He said 'Bismillah' (In the name of God) and asked the guest to start eating. Ali himself sat at the table and pretended to eat.

When Ali went to the mosque for the dawn prayer, tears of joy welled up in the eyes of the Holy Prophet.

He said, "Last night, the angels marvelled at your hospitality and an angel from God spoke of you, saying: And they give preference to others over themselves, even though they are in need."

10

Spiritual Factors

Sometimes, medicine and treatment would not work. When this happened, Fatimah would take her child's hand and go to her father. She would bring her plea for prayer to the Prophet who was the most devoted servant of God and would ask him to pray. She would say: "O Messenger of God! Pray and ask your Lord to heal your grandchild."

They would sometimes make a vow that if the children got better, they would fast or do a good deed for the sake of God and His pleasure.

In this way, in addition to physical means, they taught the children about spiritual causes and effects in the world. The children became familiar with the teachings of Islam and their spirit of servitude and sacrifice grew day by day.

The Blind Man

When the blind man reached the doorstep, Fatimah left and went inside her room. The blind man stated his needs, got what he came for, and left.

The father, who was a guest of his daughter, called out to her: "That man was blind and couldn't see you even in your home clothes."

"Dear father! He couldn't see me, but I could see him! His sense of smell was intact, he could have sensed my presence."

This modest behaviour and wise response were enough for the Prophet to say once more, "I bear witness that you are a part of me!"

72

Yearning for Paradise

What she saw, she couldn't believe. It just didn't fit with her beliefs that a father would kiss his grown daughter. Filled with questions and surprise, she went to the Prophet and asked:

"I saw you kiss Fatimah, even though she is grown up and married?!"

"Does love for a child have an age limit? Oh, Aisha! If you knew how much I love Fatimah, your love for her would grow too. Fatimah is like a heavenly being in human form. Whenever I long for the scent of Paradise, I kiss Fatimah."

73

Salman

Salman was Iranian and spoke Persian. People called him Salman the Persian! He had lived a long life, travelled extensively, and seen much of the world. He knew the luxurious lives of the daughters and wives of Persian and Roman kings up close. He was surprised by the simple lifestyle of the Prophet's daughter. He could not believe that the daughter of the highest-ranking divine messenger would wear a garment made of twelve patches of date palm fibre. He shared his memories and this surprise with the Prophet, who then spoke to his daughter.

"My father, there's nothing surprising about it. In these five years of living with Ali, our only mattress is a sheepskin that we use to keep animal feed during the day, and at night, we sleep on the same sheepskin."

74

Mishkat

One day, I asked Musa bin Ja'far for his interpretation of verse 35 of Surah al-Nur, which mentions a niche with a lamp (Mishkat fiha Misbah). He explained, "The 'Mishkat' is Fatimah, and the 'Misbah' is her two illuminating sons, Hasan and Husayn." When I queried about the phrase "as if it were a glittering star," he said, "Fatimah among the women of the world is like a shining star spreading light." Upon asking about "its oil would almost glow," he noted, "In terms of knowledge and insight, she is such that many branches of knowledge originate from her."

75

The Best for Women

"What is the best thing for women?" No one in the mosque, neither men nor women, could give a satisfactory and correct answer to the Prophet's question. Ali took the question home and asked for Fatimah's opinion.

"The best thing for women is that they should not be unnecessarily exposed to mixing with men."

The next day, Ali presented this answer to the kind and loving Prophet in the mosque. A smile of satisfaction graced his beloved face.

"Ali, why didn't you say this yesterday?"

"This answer is from your daughter."

The Prophet was overjoyed and said, "Fatimah is a part of me."

Returned from a Journey

He had just returned from a journey, and the welcome ceremony was quite bustling. He greeted everyone, but his eyes searched for someone specific. He asked for Fatimah. Whenever he travelled or returned, he would say, "I smell the delightful scent of paradise from Fatimah."

Sometimes he would also say, "The sweet scent of prophets is the smell of quince; the sweet scent of *houris* is the smell of basil; and the sweet scent of angels is the smell of flowers and tulips. But the sweet scent of Fatimah is the delightful fragrance of all three combined."

Guidance

She was young, but from her early years, she taught the women of Medina. She always encouraged them to detach from worldly desires, yet she often said, "I love three things in your world: reciting the Quran, gazing upon the face of the Prophet, and giving in the way of God."

She particularly recommended reciting certain chapters of the Quran, saying, "Whoever recites the chapters of Hadid, Waqia, and Rahman will be recognised in the heavens and on earth as one of the people of paradise."

18

Worship Schedule

She had a special worship schedule for each day, but her Thursday nights until dawn were dedicated solely to worship. She organised her home and life so she had ample time for *ibadat* and private moments with God. Hasan al-Mujtaba said, "I saw my mother, Fatimah, on the night of Friday immersed in worship. She spent the entire night in continuous bowing and prostration until the dawn began to break. At the time of dawn, I heard her naming each believer individually and praying for them."

19

Prayer for All

She raised her hands to the sky, a gesture of prayer and supplication.

The middle of the night was the perfect time. The path to heaven was open, the dominion of the *arsh* accessible, and it was time to reap the fruits of *dua*. She prayed for everyone—friends, acquaintances, neighbours, young and old. Alongside her, the children echoed each prayer with an "Amen."

After the prayer, young Hasan asked, "Mother, you prayed for everyone; but didn't you ask for anything for yourself?" With a mother's gentle touch and kindness, she replied, "My son, the neighbour first, then the home."

From a young age, she taught her children to love and wish well for others.

80

Maintaining Family Bonds

This was her constant nature and steadfast characteristic, well known to all. She kept in touch, even with those who did not visit her home. She was particularly committed to caring for and enquiring about the sick; there was never an instance she ignored.

As long as they were alive, she visited them, and when they passed away, she would stand by their graves, giving charity and sending its *thawab* and reward for the souls of the departed believers, men and women alike.

She neither forgot the living believers nor neglected those who had passed. On Mondays and Thursdays, she also visited the martyrs of Uhud to pay her respects.

Hospitality

She did not enjoy shopping at the market. She would go straight to get the necessary items. That day she bought some meat and wheat and brought them home.

Now, it was time for the lady of the house to show her skills. She put all her talent into improving the household affairs and the food, especially when they had guests.

Their guest that day was her father, the Prophet of God, and his wives.

It was the finest hospitality for the most distinguished and beloved guests. Every visitor would be honoured and respected by this household.

82

Meals & Food

The food at home was not just for the household members. There was always either a guest at their house or they sent some food to someone in need or an acquaintance.

Sometimes, she made *halwa* with oil and flour, and before they would eat, she would take it to her father, the Messenger of God, or send some to the neighbours. She loved dates and they were a regular part of their meals. She used to say, "Dates are the best gift for a believer."

83

Clothing

She did not have many clothes; however, her indoor and outdoor attire were not the same, as were her outfits for normal wear and special occasions.

Her outdoor clothes were longer and more covered, while her attire for outside gatherings was more formal. Still, all her clothes were simple and modest.

When she went to protest the confiscation of Fadak, she wore her modest outdoor clothes and a *chador* that trailed down to the ground.

84

Manners and Cleanliness

Before and after meals, she always washed her hands. She taught this to the children too. Everyone in the household made it a habit to wash their hands before sitting down for the meal and after finishing it.

They started every task with the name of God and ended it with *shukr*.

Before going to bed, they would wash their hands and perform the *wudhu* for sleep. Mother would quote Grandfather saying, "Anyone who goes to bed with greasy hands should only blame themselves [if they become ill]."

85

Aqiq

She had often seen her father combing his hair, tidying up his appearance, dyeing his hair, using *miswak*, putting on perfume, and wearing a ring on his right hand.

She had learned to groom himself at home for his spouse. He would wear his neatest clothes and best perfume for her partner.

When Ali came home, she would put on bracelets and necklaces and wear a ring on his finger. He loved *aqiq* and would say, "Anyone who wears an *aqiq* ring will always encounter goodness."

86

Father and Mother

In Ali's home, the father was a model of self-sacrifice and the mother was the embodiment of kindness and compassion; the father was a mountain of perfection, and the mother was an ocean of gentleness and beauty.

The mother would sing the many virtues of the father as lullabies and stories, teaching the children to obey their father. Likewise, when the father was present at home, he too would teach the children to respect their mother and to be well-mannered, both through his words and actions.

87

Rizq

She finished the prayer with the *salam* and started reciting the tasbih, which she had learned from his father. After the tasbih, it was time for the daily supplications and the prayers that follow the daily obligatory prayers.

These recitations were always a part of her worship routine; she would start the dawn worship with the Quran and end with a *dua*. Fatimah's eyes were never found closed at dawn.

She often reminded her children of the advice she had heard from her father: "Spend the dawn in worship and wakefulness, and witness the provision and *rizq* of the Lord."

Sincerity

"The key to solving problems lies in improving the relationship between the servant and the Almighty God and in correcting the path of servitude..."

She looked up again and scanned the crowd. The gathering had the necessary capacity, and the audience had the required understanding.

After a moment of silence, she resumed her speech. It was time to say one of those profound statements: "Whoever ascends to God with the purest form of worship, God Almighty will descend upon him with the greatest of benefits"

In other words, the more sincerely one presents their worship to the Lord, the more gracious God's provisions for them will be.

Uniting the Opposites

The new Islamic government needed constant supervision and oversight, and this responsibility fell on Ali ibn Abi Talib. Even when he was not on a mission, he would attend to the affairs of Medina, ensuring everything was in order.

In matters of Islamic law and Divine prohibitions, he was strict and firm; however, at home and among the friends of God, he was gentle and flexible.

As much as he was tender and humble with orphans and the less fortunate, he was firm and unyielding in the face of the defiant and the unjust.

90

Tasbih

In a moment, her gaze met that of the Prophet. Fatimah's modesty and the large crowd surrounding the Prophet stopped her from speaking. Without a word, she turned and left.

The next day, someone knocked on the door. The sound of the knock was familiar. She hurried to the door.

Her father entered Fatimah's home: "Zahra, my dear! Did you come to see me yesterday about something important?"

Zahra looked down. Ali spoke up:

"Fatimah has carried water until the marks have etched onto her shoulders; she's ground so much grain and baked so many loaves that her hands have become hard-skinned… I asked her to come to you to seek permission to hire a servant."

The Prophet paused for a moment.

"Would you like to learn something better than any servant?"

"Yes, why not?"

He then taught them the Tasbih of Fatimah: "After every obligatory prayer, say 'Allahu Akbar' 34 times, 'Alhamdulillah' 33 times, and 'Subhanallah' 33 times."

Lady Fatimah lifted her head and said, "I am pleased with God and His Messenger," and she repeated these words three times.

91

Hasanayn

They were like two great and complete men; their behaviour, their speech, and their manners were exemplary.

Anyone who saw them and their character would be influenced. They conducted themselves with such dignity that it was hard to believe they were just children.

Their manners were exemplary both in play and in their interactions with peers and elders. One was named Hasan and the other, Husayn. They were polite; no one ever saw the younger brother speak before the elder.

Could the children of Fatimah be anything else?

92

Call Me Father

Some called the Last Messenger by his first name, others shouted, and some spoke rudely. The angle of Revelation came with verses. It was decreed that everyone should address Muhammad with titles such as the Messenger of the Lord, the Prophet of God.

Fatimah approached her father and called out, "O Messenger of God!"

The Prophet remained silent.

"O Prophet of the Lord, O Messenger of Allah..."

Again, the Prophet was silent. Then he spoke in a soft voice:

"My daughter, dear Fatimah! This verse is not meant for you and your household. You are from me and I from you. When you call me father, it gladdens and revives my heart. God also is pleased and content. You should say, 'Father'."

93

Questions

She had many questions. The more she heard the answers, the more she felt like asking. She asked ten different questions, and each time received the complete answer. Soon, she felt too embarrassed to ask any more. She hung her head and fell silent, then asked if she could leave.

When Zahra saw the embarrassment in her eyes and knew she still wanted to ask more questions, she stopped her:

"Don't be embarrassed to ask questions."

"But I've made you tired."

"Does someone who gets a great reward for little work feel tired? I receive a reward for every answer I give you, a reward more valuable than a treasure that encompasses from the Earth to God's throne."

She did not let him leave until she had learned what she needed.

94

Special Prayer

She searched the whole house, but there was nothing to eat. It had been a few days since she and the children had a proper meal. Stepping out, she made her way to her father's house. When she met his gaze, her embarrassment kept her from speaking; however, her father read the story in his daughter's eyes. There was nothing to eat in the house of the Prophet either.

"By God! It has been a month since a fire was lit in your father's house to cook any food."

Her father did not send his daughter back empty-handed:

"Would you like me to teach you the five words that my brother, the Angel Jibra'il, has taught me?" His daughter, thirsty for this blessing, eagerly responded

"Please do!"

"Say: 'O Lord of the First and the Last, O Possessor of Mighty Strength, O Merciful to the Poor, O Most Compassionate of all the Compassionate.'"

With a smile that nestled at the corners of her lips, she returned home. Her husband, Ali, asked: "Where have you been to return so joyfully?"

"I went for the world, but I have gathered provisions for the hereafter."

That day was the best day of their lives.

95

Generosity

Outside the door stood a man in need. Lady Fatimah gave him a sheepskin coat, which he gratefully accepted. Unable to find any other precious item to give, she unclasped her necklace and handed it to the poor man, who, overjoyed, rushed to the mosque. He shared his story with the worshippers and the Prophet.

Ammar, sitting beside the Prophet, suggested that the man exchange the necklace for a camel to ride home, some clothes, food, and a bit of money. The man happily agreed. With great respect, Ammar glanced at the necklace and presented it along with a slave to the Prophet.

96

The Necklace

The door opened, and there stood the servant with the necklace in hand. "Lady, this is your necklace, and I am a gift that Ammar presented to the Prophet, and he has now bestowed upon you."

Lady Fatimah said, "I free this gift from the Prophet in the way of God. From now on, you are free, like all the free people of the world."

The servant, overwhelmed with joy and surprise, exclaimed, "What a blessed necklace; it fed the hungry, clothed the naked, provided transport to the walker, enriched the poor, freed the enslaved, and has returned to its owner."

Taking Turns

The child was thirsty. The kind grandfather stood up, milked some milk, and brought it in a clean bowl for his beloved grandchild. As Husayn approached the bowl, the grandfather stopped him and handed the bowl to Hasan instead. Zahra asked as to why the Holy Prophet acted in this manner. The Prophet's enlightening reply was:

"Both are dear to me. I gave the milk to Hasan because he asked first. Children must learn to take turns."

98

The Maid

In those times, a maid's job was to take care of all the household chores—grinding wheat, cooking, washing, sewing, etc., throughout the day and for the entire year. However, the maid in Lady Fatima's home was only responsible for half of these duties. According to her plan, one day the chores were the maid's responsibility, and the next day, they were Lady Fatima's. All tasks were divided with order, equality, and kindness; half for Lady Fatimah and half for the maid accompanied by boundless kindness!

Spoils of War

The Muslims, elated with their victory over the army of disbelievers, doubled their joy by collecting spoils. This happiness bred carelessness. Even the valley's guards forgot their commander's strict orders, lured by greed to gather more spoils. The enemy, waiting for this moment, attacked from behind.

Seventy-two of the Prophet's companions, including Hamza, the master of martyrs, swiftly joined the ranks of the heavenly ascendants. The weaker believers fled. The Prophet even called out some by name; they heard but still ran away. As always, only Ali, victor of all battles, remained to protect the Prophet's life firmly. Alone, he faced the onslaught of the disbelievers' army and scattered their united front. His body bore over eighty wounds.

This brave combat and sincere struggle was worthy of God's praise. A voice echoed in the sky: "There is no youth but Ali; there is no sword but Dhu al-Fiqar." Jibra'il, delighted in mentioning Ali, repeatedly cried out these words.

100

Nursing the Wounded

In retaliation for their defeat at the Battle of Badr and to avenge their dead, the Quraysh set out for Medina with 3000 warriors, including women like Hind, the liver-eater.

The Battle of Uhud brought deep wounds and bitter memories. Seventy-two of the Prophet's companions joined the caravan of martyrs, and many were left severely injured. Ali, without a shield, became the defender of the Prophet's life. Ali's souvenir from Uhud was over eighty injuries. The Prophet's tooth broke and his face was wounded. The bleeding wouldn't stop. Fatimah, now turned into a nurse, made her father's heart beat with joy. She burned a mat and spread its ashes on the wound, which stopped the bleeding. With that, the battle ended, but Fatimah's new task of caring for her father began.

The Essence of Virtue

"Whoever wishes to see the majesty of Israfil, the loftiness of Mika'il, and the glory of Jibra'il, let him look at my cousin Ali. In him are combined the harmony of Adam, the piety of Nuh, the friendship of Ibrahim, the supplications of Yaqub, the command of Musa, the patience of Ayyub, the asceticism of Yahya, the temperance of Isa, and the noble ethics of Muhammad." God has gathered ninety of the finest qualities of the prophets in Ali, which are found in no one else.

These are but glimpses of the high praise the greatest prophets of God have for Ali, the commander of the faithful.

Speaking of Ali

The Holy Prophet said, "Ali is with truth and truth is with Ali. Wherever Ali is, truth is there too, and it follows him wherever he goes."

He also said, "Ali is with the Qur'an, and the Qur'an is with Ali. These two shall never part until they join me at the Pool of Kawthar."

He also said, "Ali is from me, and I am from Ali; whoever insults him, insults me, and whoever insults me, insults God."

Much was spoken about Ali, his truths, his *wilayah*…

103

The Strongest Warrior

Ali was the strongest warrior among the Arabs, matching a thousand men in battle. The memory of the battle of Yalil and his victory alone against countless enemies immortalized him in history and legends.

Now, standing before the army, Amr ibn Abd Wudd chanted battle cries and tauntingly said, "Do you not believe in Paradise? Is there none among you who will send me there, or whom I shall send to hell?"

His fame in warfare, carried with it fear and the spectre of death. Each time he called out, only Ali would respond, but the Prophet denied him permission to fight three times.

Finally, the permission was given. The Lion of Islam, Mawla Haydar, with firm steps, entered the battlefield.

104

All of Faith against All of Disbelief

"O Amr! In your youth, you swore by the Kaaba that if anyone asked you for something, you would grant one of their three requests."

Amr, visibly shocked, said, "Speak your wish!"

"Convert to Islam."

He refused.

"Leave the battlefield and do not buy eternal damnation for yourself." Amr, proud, was not satisfied with retreat.

Here Ali made the third and last request, "At least fight me on foot like I do."

As the flames of combat rose between the two warriors, the battlefield scene was obscured by dust. The two armies anxiously awaited the outcome of this duel. When the dust settled,

Ali stood while Amr lay in the dust. Everyone saw that Ali had been upon Amr's chest, but he stood up, circled the field, returned, and finished Amr off.

When he recounted the story to others, he explained why he stopped for a while before killing Amr. He stopped to restrain from anger and for the sake of performing this action with absolute sincerity and *ikhlas*. It was here that the Muslims understood the secret behind the words of the Prophet when he sent Ali to fight, saying, "Islam in its entirety stands against all of disbelief."

105

Divine Trust

The Holy Prophet spoke about trust and being trustworthy, about these two precious and valuable qualities. He said, "I leave these two things with you as a trust. Be careful not to stray away from them. These two are inseparable, and so should you be; never part from them! Whoever holds on to these two will be saved, and whoever turns away will be ruined." He said, "If you cling to both, you will never be led astray. These two are equal and on the same level: the Quran and my family, my Ahl al-Bayt."

Brotherhood

Everyone found a brother; a compassionate companion, a kindred friend. Someone who would always stand by his side to form a bond of brotherhood. However, Ali was left alone. He came to the Prophet.

"O Prophet of God! No one has offered me the warm hand of brotherhood. Everyone has turned to their own dear friends."

"Ali, do not worry. You will be my friend, brother, and successor in this world and the hereafter."

The Prophet declared the bond of brotherhood. Everyone held the hand of their close friend and brother: Salman with Abu Dhar, Muhammad with Ali. And he declared, 'I am making you my brother in Allah…'

107

The Successor

The cousin of the Prophet, ibn Abbas, who was also a disciple of Ali ibn Abi Talib, said, "One day I was honoured to be in the service of the Holy Prophet. He grabbed my hand and Ali's. We reached the place we needed to be. He prayed four units of prayer. After the prayer, he raised his hands to the sky and said:

"O Lord! Just as Musa son of Imran asked for his brother Harun to be his *wazir* and partner in conveying Your message, here I am, Your prophet! I ask You to broaden my chest and ease my task. Remove the knot from my tongue so that they may understand my words, and appoint from my own family Ali ibn Abi Talib as my *wazir*. Strengthen my back through him and make him a partner in conveying my message."

At that moment, I heard the voice of a heavenly caller saying, 'O our beloved Prophet! What you have requested has been granted to you.'

108

The Mubahala

The argument went on, but when it was time to leave, they refused to accept Holy Prophet's words and called him a liar. Then they said, "If you are truthful, come and let us invoke God's curse on the liars." Initially, each was to pray, and then curse the liar; the truthful one would be saved, and the false one would suffer God's punishment. The appointed day arrived. The Christian dignitaries waited with a large crowd of followers.

As agreed, they saw the Holy Prophet, his soul Ali; the chosen woman of the Ummah Fatimah; and her two children, Hasan and Husayn, arrived for *mubahala*.

109

Radiant Faces

The leader of the Christian community had gathered distinguished members of his community and had said to them: "Today, wear your finest clothes. Present yourselves in the most beautiful manner. They should feel awe and fear of your grandeur and might."

When the Christians of Najran gathered for *mubahala* their leader said to them, "If they act like us, do not be afraid for their claims are nothing but lies."

As the sun rose, that remarkable moment approached. With eyes wide in astonishment, they saw the Prophet of Islam arriving for the *mubahala* with his close ones.

When their leader saw who had come for *mubahala* he said, "I will not agree to this *mubahala*. Steer clear of confronting these noble ones.

Accept any condition they offer. These radiant faces I see, if they ask God, He would crumble mountains for them."

110

The Needy and the Ring

He had come to the mosque, following the custom of all the needy Muslims of Medina. Some were busy with *mustahhab* prayers and others were reading the Quran. He repeated his need several times, but no one responded. It seemed he sighed and complained to God.

In a corner of the mosque, one of the worshippers gestured for him to come over and pointed to his ring.

The man was bowing in prayer. The poor man took the ring off his finger, thanked God, and left.

Jibra'il descended astonishingly quickly towards the Prophet.

"Who among you has given a ring in charity while bowing?" All the eyes turned towards Ali. Tongues declared what was revealed to the angle of revelation, a verse on the lips of the

Seal of the Prophets: "Indeed, your *wali* is God, His messenger, and those who believe, those who maintain the prayer and give charity while in *ruku*." (5:55)

A Special Verse

Jibra'il arrived with the utmost reverence, delivering a greeting from the Divine along with a verse, "Those who believe and do good deeds; truly, they are the best of creation!" (98:7)

Everyone had something to say about the verse and people speculated about its meaning.

The Holy Prophet expalined the meaning of this verse: "By the One in whose hands my soul rests: O Ali! You and your followers are the best of creation. You and your followers will come on the Day of Judgement pleased with God, and God will be pleased with you. Your enemies will come angry, their hands shackled by their necks."

Ali turned to the Prophet and posed a question:

"O Messenger! Who are my enemies?"

"Anyone who despises you and curses you."

112

The Successor

Salman, known for his thoughtful inquiries and quest for truth, was not one of the Prophet's close kin but was close enough spiritually to be considered part of his family.

He hurried to the Prophet of God to get an answer to his question.

"O Messenger of Allah! Every prophet from God has a successor. Who is yours?"

"O Salman! Who was Moses' successor?"

"Yusha son of Nun."

"And why was he the successor?"

"Because he was the most knowledgeable of his time."

With a smile and emphasis, he said:

"The successor, the keeper of my secrets, and the best man I leave behind, is the one who will fulfil my promise and govern according to my religion. And he is Ali ibn Abi Talib."

113

The Witness

Buraydah, who had been silent until that moment, listening intently, turned to Salman and said, "I also heard from the Messenger of God, 'Every prophet has a successor and heir, and know that my successor and heir is Ali.'"

(Buraydah ibn al-Husayb al-Aslami, is a companion of the Prophet who participated in most of the battles. He was the chief of the tribe of Aslam, and his conversion led many of his tribe to embrace Islam. After the Prophet's demise, he refrained from pledging allegiance to Abu Bakr, supporting Imam Ali instead.)

114

Strange Night

It seemed that night was longer than usual, souls were weary from the day's battle; yet, eyes stayed wide open, eager to see what the next day would bring.

In the battle, a deadlock had occurred. The Fortress of Qamus would not bow under the spear, arrow, and sword of the Muslim army. Early in the night, the Prophet promised the commanders victory the next day: "Tomorrow, this flag will be carried by one whom God will grant victory over the fort. He loves God and His Messenger, and God and His Messenger love him too."

Everyone wished to be the standard-bearer the next day? The sweet anticipation whirled in every soldier's mind until dawn. As the sun pierced the dark night and day settled in, all commanders who were eager to seize this distinction, hurried to the tent of the Messenger of God. The Prophet looked into the row of eager eyes.

"Where is Ali? I do not see him among you."

"He is incapacitated by eye pain."

"The victory today can only be achieved through his strong hand. Bring him, for today's flag belongs to Ali alone."

Ali the Exalted

He often emphasized, "Ali is with the truth, and the truth is with Ali. Wherever Ali is, the truth is there too. Ali is with the Quran, and the Quran is with Ali. These two will not be separated until they join me at the Pool of Kawthar."

He himself gave Ali the title "the Masih of the Ummah" and said, "Your example in my Ummah, O Ali, is like that of Isa son of Maryam; just as his people were divided into three groups: some remained faithful like the disciples, some became enemies like the Jews, and some were those who exaggerated his status, my nation will also divide into three groups regarding you: a group will be your Shia and they are the believers, a group will be your enemies who break their pledge to you, and a group are those who exaggerate your station and do *ghuluww*.

O Ali! Only you and your Shia will be in Paradise, your enemies and those who do *ghuluww* (exaggerate your station and liken you to Allah) will be in the fires of Hell."

116

Jabir

His name was Jabir, son of Abdullah, al-Ansari, one of the prominent companions of Prophet of Islam, respected by both Shia and Sunni. He once narrated, "We were learning the lessons of Divine *mari'fah* one day with the Holy Prophet of Islam. Suddenly, the Holy Prophet said something unrelated to the topic of discussion. He said, 'my brother approaches you' and everyone's gaze turned;" When the Prophet's cousin entered, he faced the Qibla, took Ali's hand, and declared, "I swear by Him in whose power my soul lies, Ali and his followers will be the saved ones on the Day of Resurrection." He paused for a moment, then continued, "Ali was the first among you to embrace faith and is the most faithful to God's covenant. He is the most just among people, and his rank is the highest with the Lord."

117

Abu al-Ghayb

A frightening and imminent defeat was looming. Rumours circulated, poisoning minds, suggesting the Prophet could not bear to see Ali, which is why he didn't bring him to Tabuk. Sorrow mingled with the Prophet's face, but God did not wish His beloved to grieve. Jibra'il arrived with news: "O Prophet! For this victory, you may choose between an army of angels or Ali ibn Abi Talib." Turning towards Medina, he cried: "O Abu al-Ghayb, assist me!"

★★★

Imam Ali at that moment was working in the palm groves with others with him. Others heard him say, 'Labbyak! Labbayak! I am at your service!' and tears welled up in his eyes as he hurriedly set off.

Ali said, "Salman! Follow me, step where I step." Salman counted the steps and followed Amir al-Mumineen — one, two, … , fifteen, sixteen, seventeen—only seventeen steps and with the help of Divine angles, they were at once in Tabuk, Ali eagerly waiting to embrace the Prophet.

118

Ghadir

Juhfa, a rest stop along the route of the Farewell Pilgrace on a Thursday, 18th Dhu al-Hijjah. In that desert heat near afternoon, the Prophet intended to speak, nearly two hours long. Jibra'il had descended by divine command: "O Messenger, proclaim what has been sent to you from your Lord..." Standing atop a *minbar* made up of saddles, he took Ali's hand, and raised it high. Now came the crucial moment as the Prophet proclaimed: "For whoever I am his *mawla,* Ali is his *mawla.*" He repeated this statement four times.

119

Last Hajj

It was the final days and the last Hajj of the Prophet. "I wish to depart from among you; but I leave behind two precious things. How will you treat them?"

The crowd erupted asking this question, "O Messenger of God! What are these two precious things?"

"One is the Book of God, and the other is my family, my Ahl al-Bayt. God has informed me that these two shall never part from each other. Do not precede them nor stay behind them, for you would be doomed."

Completion of Religion

The Holy Prophet grabbed Ali's hand and raised it. Thereafter he joined the fingers of his other hand and said, "Just like these two fingers, the Book of God and my Ahl al-Bayt are together and will not be separated until they join me by the Pond of Kawthar. Stay with them, and you will not be misled."

After the sermon, they stepped down from the *minbar* together; the Prophet with his successor. He then commanded all present, men and women, to pledge allegiance to Ali as the Imam and Caliph, referring to him as Amir al-Mu'mineen.

The Happiest Day for Fatimah

Men pledged allegiance by placing their hands in the Imam's, offering congratulations. Women, from the other side, dipped their hands in water, pledging and then offering their felicitations.

The scribes of Divine revelation and those who had memorized the Quran were summoned.

The Lord recorded the day of Ali's appointment in the Quran: "Today, I have perfected your religion for you, completed My favour upon you, and have chosen for you Islam as your religion."

That day was the happiest day for Fatimah al-Zahra.

122

Spiritual Parents

That day the women of Medina were very eager to ask questions. A multitude of questions came to the Prophet's daughter; her presence was a precious opportunity, extensively used by the women of Medina to ask numerous questions.

She answered each inquirer with utmost patience and detail, ensuring satisfaction before moving to the next question.

While answering one of the questions, she pointed out the importance of the allegiance to the Divine guides: "Prefer the satisfaction of your spiritual parents over that of your physical parents, for while the former can secure the latter's approval, the other way round is not always possible."

Certainly, both the Prophet and Ali were the spiritual fathers of the Muslim Ummah.

That is why in one narration the Holy Prophet said, "I and Ali are fathers of this Ummah."

SECTION FOUR

Longing

for

the Beloved

123

Bitter Smile

It was a story of sorrowful separation, a tale of the departure of the dearest of companions. The loss was immense, and tears, the smallest comfort. Amidst the crying, a smile blossomed unexpectedly.

While the tears were evident, holding no secret; that smile, why was it there?

The father had said, "You are the first of my kin to join me."

Remembering death and the early reunion with her father was a solace amid the grief for Fatimah.

124

The Scribe of Revelation

When the Prophet passed away, Ali was filled with concern. He feared the deceit of the hypocrites, aiming to divide the Muslims. More than anything, he worried about the distortion of the Quran, that it might become a tool for conflict among Muslims. He vowed not to don his cloak until he had gathered the Quran with its interpretation and commentary.

He stayed out of sight for days, recording on paper all that he had heard from the blessed tongue of his Prophet.

Now, Ali was the first scribe of revelation, the first to write down the Quran along with its interpretation, explaining the reasons and events that triggered the revelation of its verses.

125

The Nightly Invitation

At night, Fatimah, Hasan and Husayn led by Ali, would visit the homes of the people of Medina.

Fatimah would remind them of the words of the Prophet, especially about Ghadir, where they were present; yet none responded.

From one house to another, whenever they faced disappointment, they moved on. One by one, she spoke to the Ansar and Muhajireen, presenting evidence and reminding them of narrations of the Holy Prophet.

Near dawn, from all those present at Ghadir, only four agreed to testify that Ali was rightful.

The Final Moments

Her house was always clean and tidy.

She placed great importance on the cleanliness of the home, even more so on the tidiness of the children.

Nothing deterred her from fulfilling the duties she was entrusted with.

Knowing she had but a short time left in this transient world, she cleaned the house as usual, prepared the food, and completed her household works. She arranged her bed to face the Qibla, ready to meet her creator with a peaceful heart when the moment death would arrive.

127

Tearful Eyes

Ali's eyes were full of tears when he saw the state of Fatimah.

She opened her eyes. As her gaze met Ali's, her beautiful eyes also clouded with tears.

"Dear Fatimah! Why do you cry? It is me who will have to bear separation from you."

"Dear Ali! I do not weep for my own sorrow. My tears are for you and all the hardships ahead. For the injustice you will face and the times when Zahra is not by your side to help you."

128

Peace

Fatimah was a source of peace for Ali. Now that she was leaving, she took the tranquillity with her. Zahra's grief stirred the sea-like heart of Mawla Ali into a storm.

He wept quietly, recalling the good days spent with Zahra: "By God! In our life together, I never angered Fatimah, nor did I compel her to do anything until she left this world, afflicting me with the pain of her absence.

She, too, never angered me and never went against my wish in her actions. Whenever I looked at her, no matter how deep my sorrow, it would be washed away from my heart."

Memories of the Beloved

Revisiting cherished memories was the companion of his lonely nights. At times, his solitude was filled with thoughts of Zahra, while at other times, he would cool his burning heart by speaking to the well.

Occasionally, he spoke of the pleasant past and Zahra's virtues with close companions: "Fatimah lived with me the best of lives; she would draw water with the leather bucket so much that it left marks on her hands. She would ground flour with the millstone till her fingers were calloused. She would sweep the house until her clothes would become dusty, and she would collect wood for the fire until her clothes would become soiled."

Beloved of God

That year it did not rain enough and there was a drought. It was year in which the rain had abandoned everyone. The people were worried and turned to prayer, but no prayers were answered. They looked for someone with a connection to the Heavens and approached Ali

"Master! Please pray so that by your status near Allah, our prayers will not be rejected."

When Imam Ali's hands became raised in supplication, the sky generously poured its bounty.

Everyone knew how beloved and close Ali was to the Lord of the skies.

131

Complaint

The judge of the court, the second Caliph, was hearing a complaint against Ali made by one of the people of Medina.

"O Abu al-Hasan! Stand next to the complainant so that I can attend to his complaint."

The Master of the Faithful stood up, though signs of unhappiness were visible on his face.

"What happened, O Abu al-Hasan? Did my asking you to stand by the complainant upset you?"

His reply was noteworthy:

"You called the complainant by his name and me by my *kunyah*; this is not justice! Perhaps he might feel intimidated by your behaviour and respect towards me."

132

Slave Girl and the Dates

"This girl has no choice; she is a slave. Her master is not satisfied with the dates she bought. Please return her money and take back your dates."

The shop owner didn't know who he was speaking to! He refused to listen and spoke harshly, striking Ali on the chest...

From the frowns and gestures of the people around, he realized he was standing before Imam Ali; the Caliph of the Muslims who often visited the market to check on things.

He was terrified. He quickly returned the girl's money and ran towards the Imam:

"Master, forgive me and be pleased with me!"

"I will not be pleased until you correct your behaviour, uphold people's rights, and implement manners and morality in your life."

133

Ibadat of Ali

It was more than love; it was like being entirely submerged in Divine beauty. Whenever he found the time, he would stand in prayer.

While performing a *mustahhab* prayer, he was so detached from this worldly realm that the arrow embedded in his leg bone which had been tormenting him, could no longer be felt.

His son Hasan suggested that they remove the arrow during these moments when Ali is connect to his Lord.

The son knew his father well, understanding that only during prayer was Ali truly not of this world. They seized the moment and removed the arrow; and indeed the arrow was removed without Ali feeling the pain!

134

This Ill-Omened Hour

They were heading towards Nahrawan, and the Khawarij accepted no advice. Their only guide to the righteous path was the raw sword. As the moment to depart arrived, suddenly the voice of someone rushing near was heard:

"Do not go... do not go... this hour is not good."

He had studied astrology and could tell the fortunate and unfortunate times by the stars. Now, he was hurrying towards Imam Ali...

"O Commander of the Faithful! Do not start this journey now; I fear you will face defeat. The stars say: ...."

Ali interrupted him and said, "Whoever believes these words from you has denied the Quran and sought independence from God for assistance in his affairs!"

By God's will, no battle had ever been so decisively victorious for Ali like the battle of Nahrawan.

Three Conditions for Hosting

Hopeful and honoured, he invited him to be his guest, thinking, "What greater honour is there than to host Ali?"

He accepted, but not without conditions.

"There are three conditions. If you agree, I will come."

Not wanting to miss this great honour, he agreed.

"First, whatever you have at home is fine; don't buy anything from outside. Second, do not hold back anything you have. Third, do not give trouble to your wife and children."

Ali did not want the host to have any bad memories of the visit.

136

Battle of Siffin

The army, tired and thirsty from the journey, found the enemy blocking access to water. He wrote to Mu'awiyah, "I do not wish to fight before talking and resolving matters with you through negotiations. However, your troops have started the fight, attacking our scouts and blocking access to the Euphrates, setting the path for conflict."

Mu'awiyah did not respond to the letter. The Imam ordered an attack. The Muslim army won. After waiting several days, Ali's companions now controlled the water. Some suggested denying the enemy water in return.

A frown crossed his brow as he said, "God has made water permissible for both the believer and the non-believer. Withholding it from others is neither noble nor manly, especially now that God has granted you victory and repelled their aggression."

137

Looking at the Sky

In the midst of battle, his varying gazes caught my eye. At one moment, he focused on the enemy; at another, he looked anxiously towards the sky.

I couldn't resist and approached him, "My master! I wish to know the secret behind this behaviour; why do you sometimes stop fighting and stare at the sky?"

He replied, "The day has reached mid-point, and the time for prayer is near. I do not want to miss the prayer at its prescribed time."

138

Insults

They were exchanging insults; curse for curse. Ali quickly reached his companions:

"Why do you act this way?"

"The enemies started it..."

"Insults are the words of someone without a valid argument. You are people of reason. The Quran is among you. Speak with logic, evidence, and proof."

No one, not even Mu'awiyah, the toughest and vilest of enemies, received his curse. He said, "We have come to revive the religion; why should we allow ourselves to be distracted by petty and worthless actions?"

140

Justice of Ali

Walking through the streets of Kufa, he praised Ali while the fingers were severed from his hand.

"Who severed these fingers?"

"This is the sign of Ali's justice."

Despite my astonishment, he continued to praise Ali, even with a severed hand.

"Why would I not? I stole, and this was my deserved punishment and it has purified me from sin."

141

Believer and Hypocrite

Ali said to ibn Kawwa, "The Prophet told me, 'If you cut a believer into pieces, his affection towards you will only increase. If you pour honey into the mouth of a hypocrite, his enmity will not lessen.'"

***

He sent his son Hasan after the man whose fingers were cut.

"I severed your hand, and you praise me?"

"The God of the universe praises you. Who am I to do otherwise?"

"May your path no longer veer towards wrong."

He draped his cloak of kindness over the man's hand, recited a *dua*, and by Divine

grace his fingers returned. The man walked
home again, head held high with love for Ali
and marked by his kindness.

142

The Value of Government

The army was camped in Dhi Qar, preparing for the Battle of Camel. One of the commanders had to report to Ali and so he went early in the morning to his tent. He asked for permission and entered the commander in chief's tent. He was seated, repairing his torn shoes.

Commander in chief Ali asked, "O son of Abbas! How much are these shoes worth?"

What was he to say? A pair of worn-out sandals!

"Almost nothing. They have no value."

"For me, ruling over you all is worth less than these torn shoes; unless I can establish a right or eradicate a wrong and enforce justice."

143

A Difficult Question

Ali knew that people didn't know the way and were unaware. He held a sea of knowledge within him. He didn't want them to remain in ignorance and suffer. He often said, "I am more familiar with the ways of the heavens than the earth." He felt passionate and often exclaimed, "Ask me before you lose me!"

However, how unfortunate it was that someone asked him, "Tell me, how many hairs are in my beard?!" Ali spent time even with such people.

When he said, "By the Lord of the Kaaba, I have succeeded!" it meant he had found salvation and relief from those who embraced ignorance.

144

The Last Will

The poison of Ibn Muljam's sword had done its job, and the doctor's predictions were right. Orphans stood outside the house, holding milk. In his last will to Hasan and Husayn, he expressed his concern for the people: "I advise you two, all my children and family, and anyone who hears my words, to fear God, maintain discipline, and make peace among people...I enjoin you with regards to orphans...

I enjoin you with regards to your neighbours...I enjoin you with regards to the Qur'an... I enjoin you with regards to the prayers...

It was our master Ali who drank half the milk and give the other half...to your killer?!"